Lemon Tea Cake

1½ cups flour
1 t. baking powder
½ t. salt
½ c. unsalted butter, softened

1 c. granulated sugar
2 large eggs
½ cup milk
Grated zest and juice of 1 lemon

Preheat the oven to 325°. Grease an 8½ x 4 inch loaf pan. In a small bowl, stir together the flour, baking powder

Happy Birthday!

Love,
Bill & Sue

1995

*A cakewalk is a promenade in which the couple
performing the most intricate steps wins a cake as their prize.*

Cakewalk

Loving Spoonfuls From a Southern Kitchen

25 CAKE RECIPES
WRITTEN AND ILLUSTRATED BY

Robbin Gourley

DOUBLEDAY

NEW YORK LONDON TORONTO SYDNEY AUCKLAND

Published by DOUBLEDAY

a division of Bantam Doubleday Dell Publishing Group, Inc.

1540 Broadway, New York, New York 10036

DOUBLEDAY and the portrayal of an anchor with a dolphin are trademarks

of Doubleday, a division of Bantam Doubleday Dell Publishing Group, Inc.

LIBRARY OF CONGRESS CATALOGING-IN-PUBLICATION DATA

Gourley, Robbin.

Cakewalk : loving spoonfuls from a Southern kitchen : 25 cake

recipes / written and illustrated by Robbin Gourley.—1st ed.

p.   cm.

ISBN 0-385-47174-2

1. Cake.   I. Title.

TX771.G68   1994

641.8'653—dc20   94-15251

CIP

Book Design by Robbin Gourley

Calligraphy by Bernard Maisner

Printed in Italy

October 1994

First Edition

1 3 5 7 9 10 8 6 4 2

FOR JEFF

SPECIAL THANKS TO

Master baker, Ford Rogers,
Diane Botnick, script doctor sine qua non,
Lisa Sloane, my tireless, enthusiastic design support;
Schellie Hagan for her rogue smarts,
Bernard Maisner, artist and calligrapher,
Susan Ginsburg for all her wisdom,
and Judy Kern for her steadfast editorial presence.

CONTENTS

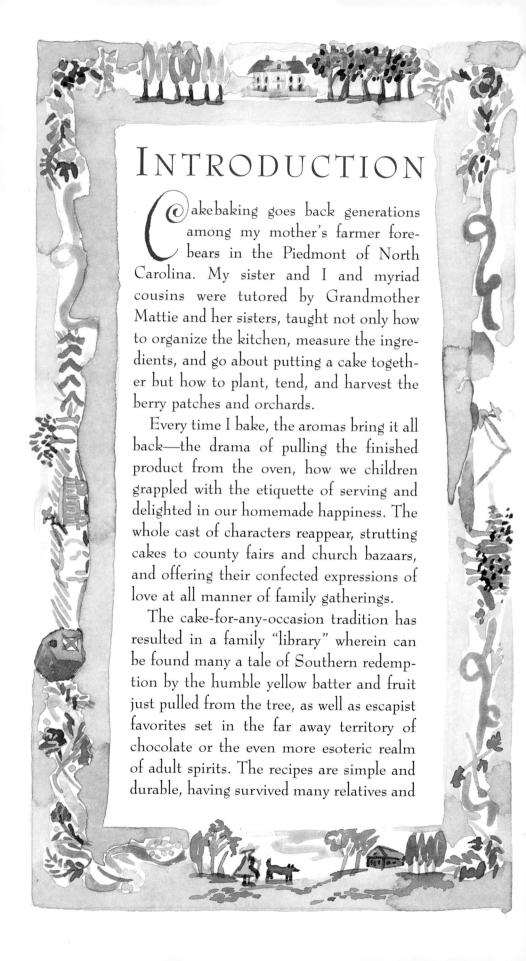

INTRODUCTION

Cakebaking goes back generations among my mother's farmer fore-bears in the Piedmont of North Carolina. My sister and I and myriad cousins were tutored by Grandmother Mattie and her sisters, taught not only how to organize the kitchen, measure the ingredients, and go about putting a cake together but how to plant, tend, and harvest the berry patches and orchards.

Every time I bake, the aromas bring it all back—the drama of pulling the finished product from the oven, how we children grappled with the etiquette of serving and delighted in our homemade happiness. The whole cast of characters reappear, strutting cakes to county fairs and church bazaars, and offering their confected expressions of love at all manner of family gatherings.

The cake-for-any-occasion tradition has resulted in a family "library" wherein can be found many a tale of Southern redemption by the humble yellow batter and fruit just pulled from the tree, as well as escapist favorites set in the far away territory of chocolate or the even more esoteric realm of adult spirits. The recipes are simple and durable, having survived many relatives and

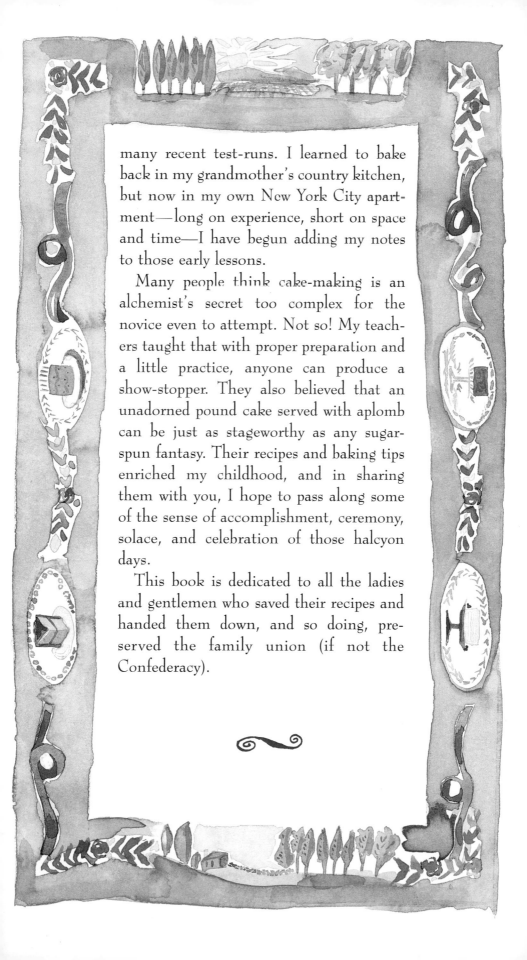

many recent test-runs. I learned to bake back in my grandmother's country kitchen, but now in my own New York City apartment—long on experience, short on space and time—I have begun adding my notes to those early lessons.

Many people think cake-making is an alchemist's secret too complex for the novice even to attempt. Not so! My teachers taught that with proper preparation and a little practice, anyone can produce a show-stopper. They also believed that an unadorned pound cake served with aplomb can be just as stageworthy as any sugar-spun fantasy. Their recipes and baking tips enriched my childhood, and in sharing them with you, I hope to pass along some of the sense of accomplishment, ceremony, solace, and celebration of those halcyon days.

This book is dedicated to all the ladies and gentlemen who saved their recipes and handed them down, and so doing, preserved the family union (if not the Confederacy).

CAKEBAKING TIPS

- Preheat the oven before baking a cake.

- Grease pans with unsalted butter, margarine, or shortening—never oil.

- Bake layers in the center of the oven, with pans not touching each other or the oven walls (unless the recipe says otherwise).

- Start testing layers for doneness at the shortest suggested cooking time.

- A cake is done when a wire tester or toothpick inserted near the center of the cake comes out dry with no crumbs clinging to it, or when the cake springs back when pressed lightly in the center with a finger.

- When baking two or more layers, test each one for doneness. Layers in the back of the oven may be ready 2 to 5 minutes before those in the front. Remove each layer as it tests done.

- After cooling on a rack, flip the cake layer onto a plate or your hand, and slowly and carefully pull the rack away.

- Cool the cake completely before frosting, but frost it as soon as it is cool. If the cake sits too long before frosting, it will begin to dry out.

- Softened butter means butter at room temperature. You can hasten softening by placing butter in the microwave for about 45 seconds at a third of the power (ovens vary). Allow it to sit for an additional 2 minutes.

- Bring eggs quickly to room temperature by setting them in a bowl of warm water for several minutes.

- Have all ingredients at room temperature before mixing a cake (unless otherwise indicated).

- Tread lightly and avoid major activity in the kitchen while cakes are baking.

- Measure dry ingredients by measuring cup or spoon. Scrape off excess with a straight edge, such as the back of a knife. If a recipe calls for sifting before measuring, sift into a bowl, then proceed with measuring.

- A store-bought sifter is not necessary for sifting. Place the ingredients in a wire strainer, hold at an angle over a bowl, and tap the upper edge of the strainer with a spoon or knife.

- Test the oven temperature for accuracy. Inexpensive oven thermometers are often not accurate. Use reputable gauges, or more than one, or have your service agent test your oven.

- Separate eggs while cold, then bring them to room temperature.

- Brush loose crumbs from layers before frosting.

- To keep the plate clean, arrange strips of wax paper under the cake edges while frosting. Remove carefully.

- When frosting two-layer cakes, spread about a quarter of the frosting between the layers. For three-layer cakes, use the same amount but spread it thinner.

- Have all ingredients measured, mixed, sifted, and prepared before you start to assemble a cake, so as to have as little delay as possible between steps.

- When folding in egg whites, fold in a quarter to a third first to thin the batter, then fold in the remaining whites. This method causes less deflation than folding all at once. Use a balloon whisk, a large spoon, or large rubber spatula, and cut through the center of the batter; bring the utensil up the side of the bowl, literally folding the batter into itself. Turn the bowl slightly and repeat until no clumps of white can be seen. Don't overfold!

- Use only the pan size and shape designated in the recipe. Different-size pans can cause overflow, or not allow proper rising or browning.

- Pans that have been heated on the stove (for melting chocolate, thickening frosting bases, etc.) can be brought to room temperature quickly by setting them in cold water in a bowl or the kitchen sink. Do not do this with glass pans.

- Always use "large" eggs (unless otherwise stipulated).

- To keep damp or oily ingredients, such as raisins or nuts, from clumping together, toss them with a little of the recipe's flour before adding to the batter.

- Because of salmonella contamination, licking the bowl or spoon of batter containing raw eggs is not a good idea. If you're making a cake or frosting that doesn't contain eggs, lick away.

- When mixing or beating anything with an electric mixer, scrape down the sides of the bowl and the beaters regularly.

- Alcohol evaporates when cooked, leaving the essence. In the recipes calling for spirits, you may adjust the amount to taste.

- Vegetable shortening, like Crisco, the bane of modern nutritionists, must be used when called for to ensure a lighter textured cake. There are no substitutions.

Sometime in 1912,
Arnet Ireland
began walking the
seven long miles to
town to sit with
Miss Mattie Gibson
in her family's parlor.

One afternoon he was
served the jam cake
Mattie had made
that morning.

Call it coincidence,
she'd say, but
that was the day
he asked for her hand.

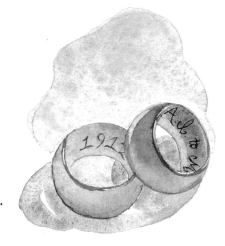

Jam Cake

The jam in the frosting tints this wonderful cake pastel mauve.
The effect with berries ringed round the top is lovely.

Cake

3½ cups unbleached, all-purpose
    flour
1   teaspoon baking soda
2   teaspoons baking powder
½   teaspoon salt
2   teaspoons ground cinnamon
1   teaspoon grated nutmeg
1   teaspoon ground allspice
½   teaspoon ground cloves

1   cup buttermilk
2   tablespoons lemon juice
1½ cups seedless blackberry or
    raspberry jam
4   large eggs
1   cup (2 sticks) unsalted butter,
    softened
1½ cups granulated sugar

Preheat the oven to 350°F. Grease and flour two 9-inch cake pans.

In a bowl, sift together the flour, baking soda, baking powder, salt, and spices. Set aside.

In another bowl, thoroughly whisk together the buttermilk, lemon juice, jam, and eggs. Set aside.

In a large bowl, with an electric mixer or by hand, cream together the butter and sugar until fluffy. Alternately, add some of the dry and liquid ingredients to the butter and sugar mixture, beating well after each addition. When everything is incorporated, pour the batter into the pans, smooth the tops, and bake for 35 minutes, or until the cake tests done. Cool in the pans for 10 minutes, then invert onto racks. Cool completely before frosting.

Frosting

One 16-ounce box confectioners'
    sugar
6   tablespoons unsalted butter,
    softened
½   cup seedless blackberry or
    raspberry jam

2–3 teaspoons blackberry liqueur,
    Chambord (a sweet raspberry
    liquor), crème de cassis, or
    vanilla extract
Fresh blackberries or raspberries for
    garnish, in season

Place the confectioners' sugar, butter, jam, and 2 teaspoons of liqueur or extract in a large bowl. With an electric mixer or by hand, beat until smooth. If too thick, add more liqueur or extract until a spreading consistency is achieved.

Frost the cake. Decorate with fresh berries, if desired.

Homemade jam is not essential for success
here, but it does feel good to say you made the whole thing.

I remember days on the farm ~ just
Grandmother Mattie and I ~ when comfort
was the only answer to some unasked question.
A gingerbread day ~ and we'd start baking.
I remember how proud I felt being called
her No. 1 bowl-licker, how the whole house
cozied with the smell of spice, and her
look of satisfaction as she pulled our creation
out of the oven, blew away the steam, and
awarded me the first bite.

Gingerbread

*This American innovation is bliss when warm from the oven and
served with a generous dollop of whipped cream.*

Cake

½ cup crystallized ginger
2 cups unbleached flour
½ teaspoon baking soda
¼ teaspoon salt
½ teaspoon finely ground black
   pepper
1 teaspoon ground ginger
1 teaspoon ground cinnamon
½ teaspoon grated nutmeg

¼ teaspoon ground cloves
6 tablespoons unsalted butter
½ cup firmly packed dark brown
   sugar
½ cup molasses
¼ cup water
2 large eggs
¼ cup bourbon (optional)

Preheat the oven to 350°F. Grease an 8-inch square cake pan.

Place the crystallized ginger in the bowl of a food processor fitted with a
steel blade and process until pureed. (It will stick to the sides of the processor.)
Alternatively, you may chop the ginger very fine by hand.

In a bowl, sift together the flour, baking soda, salt, and spices. Set aside.

In a small saucepan, melt the butter. Remove it from the heat, stir in the
brown sugar and molasses, then stir in the water. Transfer the mixture to a
large mixing bowl. Beat in the ginger puree, then the eggs. Add bourbon, if
desired. Add the flour/spice mixture and mix only until thoroughly moistened
and evenly colored.

Pour the batter into the pan and bake for 45 to 50 minutes, or until a
toothpick inserted in the center comes out clean.

Let cool until warm or room temperature before serving. Serve the cake
from the pan or invert onto a plate or baking sheet, and reinvert onto a serving plate. Store leftovers in plastic wrap.

Topping (optional)

1 cup heavy cream

2 tablespoons confectioners' sugar
2 tablespoons bourbon (optional)

In a small bowl, beat the cream until the beater marks show. Add the sugar
and bourbon and beat until stiff peaks form. Chill until ready to serve on the
gingerbread.

*⊚ If it's adults you're aiming to please, spoon or brush ¼ cup bourbon over the top of
the cake immediately after removing it from the oven.*

The eggs of guinea hens were said to be extra rich in taste and texture, and for Mattie's pound cake, baked weekly, only the best would do. From the hayloft we could scout the hens' nests, which were randomly scattered across the grassy fields. Gathering the wild eggs was much more fun than being sent to fetch from the smelly coop.

Mattie's Pound Cake

*Sliced, sugared peaches will transform this plain Jane
into an elegant confection.*

Cake

3   cups all-purpose flour
½   teaspoon baking powder
¼   teaspoon salt
1   cup milk
1½ teaspoons lemon extract
½   teaspoon vanilla extract

1   cup (2 sticks) unsalted butter,
    softened
½   cup vegetable shortening
    (Crisco)
3   cups granulated sugar
5   large eggs

Preheat the oven to 325°F. Grease a 10-inch tube or bundt pan.
In a bowl, sift together the flour, baking powder, and salt. Set aside.
Combine the milk and the extracts. Set aside.

In a mixing bowl, cream together the butter, shortening, and sugar until
light and fluffy. Add half the milk mixture and blend well. Beginning with the
flour mixture, alternately add some flour and the eggs, one at a time, beating
well after each addition. Add the rest of the milk mixture. Mix until combined.

Pour the batter into the pan and bake for 1 hour 30 minutes, or until a
toothpick inserted in the center comes out clean. Turn out onto a rack to
cool completely.

*Rich, moist, you'll dub this one the long-keeper. Slice thin and toast for breakfast or
an afterschool snack. Or slice, bag, and freeze for heating
a-piece-at-a-time in the toaster.*

Bake this cake for:

8 hearty gentlemen;

12 petite ladies;

10 large teenagers;

16 little children.

Sweet Potato Cake

*A nice change from carrot cake, and still packing a dose of vitamin A,
this one's a favorite with both children and adults.*

Cake

2 cups (about 1 pound) finely grated, peeled raw sweet potatoes
1/4 cup lemon juice
1 cup whole wheat flour
1 cup sifted cake flour
2 teaspoons baking powder
1 teaspoon baking soda
1/2 teaspoon salt
1 teaspoon ground cinnamon

1/2 teaspoon ground ginger
1/2 teaspoon grated nutmeg
1 cup vegetable oil
1 1/2 cups firmly packed light brown sugar
4 large eggs
1 1/2 teaspoons vanilla extract
1 cup chopped pecans

Preheat the oven to 350°F. Grease and flour two 9-inch cake pans.

Grate the sweet potatoes and combine with the lemon juice to prevent darkening. Set aside.

In a bowl, sift together the flours, baking powder, baking soda, salt, and spices. Set aside.

In a large mixing bowl, beat together the oil and sugar. Add the eggs and beat until smooth and honey-colored. Mix in the sweet potatoes, then the dry ingredients, and beat until thoroughly moistened. Add the vanilla extract and pecans and mix well.

Divide the batter equally between the pans and bake for 30 to 35 minutes, or until each layer springs back when lightly touched in the center.

Cool for 10 minutes in the pans, then turn out and cool completely on racks.

Roasted Pecan Frosting

1½ cups pecan halves

¼ cup (½ stick) unsalted butter, softened

8 ounces cream cheese, at room temperature

2½ cups confectioners' sugar, sifted

¼ teaspoon salt

1 teaspoon vanilla extract

Spread the nuts on a baking sheet and roast in the 350°F. oven (after the cake is removed), stirring occasionally, for 10 to 12 minutes, or until lightly browned. Remove the nuts from the pan and cool to room temperature.

In the bowl of a food processor fitted with a steel blade, process the nuts until ground very fine. Add the butter and continue to process, scraping down the sides of the bowl a couple of times until the mixture resembles a molasses/cornmeal paste.

Combine the nut paste and cream cheese in a bowl. Beat until well mixed. Add the sugar, salt, and vanilla extract, and beat until smooth.

Spread the frosting between the layers and on the top and sides of the cake.

☙ To vary the look, instead of icing the top and sides of the cake, ice only between the layers. Place a simple doily or your own stencil on the top layer and sift confectioners' sugar liberally through it for a lacy after effect.

RISE AND SHINE

My dad is a master baker – in a tradition all his own – his concise repertoire perfected and sumptuous. He used to get up early, just to bake this specialty. "Rise and shine," he'd shout from the bottom of the stairs, pulling us instantaneously from our beds for a breakfast of sunnyside upside-down cake.

Rise and Shine Cake

[Pineapple Upside-Down Cake]

A zingy mixture of fruit and nuts starts out on the bottom but winds up on top as a glorious glaze.

Cake

One 20-ounce can sliced pineapple in its own juice

10 tablespoons (1¼ sticks) unsalted butter, softened

⅔ cup firmly packed dark brown sugar

Pecans, or fresh or candied cherries (optional)

½ cup granulated sugar

2 cups sifted cake flour

2 teaspoons baking powder

¼ teaspoon salt

2 large eggs

1 teaspoon vanilla extract

Whipped cream (optional)

Drain the pineapple, reserving the juice.

Preheat the oven to 350°F.

Heat a 10-inch cast-iron skillet on top of the stove. Melt 6 tablespoons of the butter in it. Remove from the heat. Sprinkle the brown sugar evenly over the bottom of the skillet. Arrange as many drained whole pineapple slices as will fit in the pan. To make an attractive design use pecans or fresh or candied cherries between and in the holes of the pineapple slices.

In a mixing bowl, combine the remaining 4 tablespoons of butter, the granulated sugar, flour, baking powder, salt, eggs, vanilla extract, and ¾ cup of the reserved pineapple juice. Mix on low until moistened. At high speed, beat for 2 minutes, scraping the sides and bottom of the bowl several times.

Pour the batter over the pineapple slices. Bake for 40 minutes, or until a toothpick inserted in the center of the cake comes out clean.

Cool for 5 minutes. Cover with a serving plate. Flip over and let sit a few seconds before carefully removing from the pan.

Serve warm or at room temperature, plain or with whipped cream.

NOTE: For adults only, before baking, place drained pineapple slices in a shallow dish and pour ⅓ cup very dark rum (such as Myers's) over them. Cover and set aside for 1 to 4 hours, turning the slices over a few times. Take out the pineapple slices and reserve the rum. Bake as above. Immediately upon removing the cake from the oven, drizzle or spoon reserved rum over the top.

⊚ The cast-iron skillet, mainstay of Southern cooks, ensures the caramelizing of the brown sugar.

On the first fallish Saturday of the year, we'd help pack a picnic and then pile into the blue Ford station wagon for a long drive up into the Great Smoky Mountains. This cake always traveled well (a lot better than we did, I'm told), but never made it back home.

Chocolate Pound Cake
[The Good Traveler]

A comfort cake, rich, tender, and chocolate, this one evokes a whiff of home with every baking.

Cake

¼	cup strong coffee	6	large eggs
4	ounces unsweetened chocolate, coarsely chopped (See note.)	1	teaspoon baking powder
		¼	teaspoon baking soda
1	cup (2 sticks) unsalted butter	¼	teaspoon salt
3	cups granulated sugar	1	cup sour cream
3	cups sifted unbleached all-purpose flour	1½	teaspoons vanilla extract

Preheat the oven to 325°F. Grease and flour a 10-inch tube pan.

In a small saucepan, heat the coffee until it just begins to boil around the edges. Remove from the heat, add the chocolate, cover, and set aside for 5 minutes.

After 5 minutes, stir the chocolate/coffee mixture until smooth. It will thicken as you stir, ending up a mashed-potatolike texture. Test it with your finger. If it's barely warm to the touch, proceed. If not, wait until it cools.

Place the butter and the chocolate/coffee mixture in a large bowl. Beat with an electric mixer or by hand until the ingredients are well combined. Add the sugar and continue to cream together thoroughly. (The mixture will be grainy at this point.) Add the eggs, one at a time, beating well after each addition.

In a small bowl, sift together the flour, baking powder, baking soda, and salt.

In another small bowl, combine the sour cream and vanilla extract.

Add a quarter of the dry ingredients to the creamed mixture, beating thoroughly, then a quarter of the sour cream, alternating until all the ingredients are combined.

Pour the batter into the pan and smooth the top. Bake for 1 hour 20 minutes, or until the cake springs back when lightly touched. Allow to cool for 15 minutes in the pan, then unmold and cool completely before slicing or drizzling with the brandy glaze. Store in a tightly closed container.

Brandy Glaze (optional)

1½ cups confectioners' sugar
2 tablespoons unsalted butter, melted

2–3 tablespoons brandy, Cognac, or vanilla extract

Put the sugar and butter in a small bowl, stirring to combine as well as possible. Add the brandy gradually, whisking until the mixture reaches the consistency you desire. (Don't thin it too much.) Spoon the icing over the cake, allowing it to drip down the sides.

NOTE: You can substitute ½ cup cocoa and ¼ cup additional butter for the chocolate. Cream the butter with the cup of butter for the cake. Sift the cocoa with the dry ingredients. The result is less chocolatey, but still delicious.

Often we had tea at Miss Ayer's. We'd sit beneath an enormous chandelier, all dressed up and watching for the moment when she would tap a button on the floor with her dainty foot. In through the swinging door an aproned maid would parade a perfect cake on a silver tray!

The pleasure of this sweet cake was undiminished even under the strain of behaving one's best.

Lemon Tea Cake

Steeped in a heavenly lemon sauce, this simple pound is the doyenne of Southern tea cakes.

Cake

1⅔ cups all-purpose flour
1   teaspoon baking powder
½   teaspoon salt
½   cup (1 stick) unsalted butter, softened

1   cup granulated sugar
2   large eggs
½   cup milk
Grated zest and juice of 1 lemon

Preheat the oven to 325°F. Grease an 8½ by 4½-inch loaf pan.

In a small bowl, stir together the flour, baking powder, and salt. Set aside.

In a mixing bowl, cream together the butter and sugar. Add the eggs, one at a time, beating well after each addition. Add some of the flour mixture and some of the milk alternately, mixing well after each addition, until both are incorporated. Add the lemon zest and lemon juice. Mix thoroughly.

Pour the batter into the prepared pan, smoothing out the top. Bake for 55 minutes to 1 hour, or until a toothpick inserted in the center comes out clean. Cool in the pan on a rack for 10 minutes.

Glaze

1   cup sifted confectioners' sugar   Juice of 1 lemon

In a small bowl, combine the sugar and lemon juice.

Pour over the cake 10 minutes after it's removed from the oven. Allow the glaze to run down between the cake and the sides of the pan. Cool for 15 more minutes. Cover with a plate and invert. Remove the cake pan. Cover with a serving plate and invert again. Serve warm or at room temperature.

☺ *Best Iced Tea: Use four orange pekoe tea bags. Bring 1½ quarts of water to a rolling boil. Turn off the water and add the tea bags. Steep covered for 3 minutes—not more than 4. WATCH THE CLOCK! Oversteeping will make the tea bitter. Remove the tea bags; sweeten to taste. Allow to cool, pour over ice, and add lemon to taste.*

A long, slow day would lead me to Aunt Florence's. She had a bowl of nonpareils and stories from the North, where she grew up. The only Yankee among us, she had to commit some fancy cakery to compete. She did all right with this one. It has a sophisticated taste (being from the North, you know).

Divine Marble Cake

[Touch of the North]

*Dark chocolate swirls through this alluring cake, seducing
the eye as well as the taste buds.*

Cake

3	cups all-purpose flour	2½	cups granulated sugar
¼	teaspoon salt	6	large eggs
¼	teaspoon baking soda	1	cup sour cream
6	ounces semisweet chocolate	2	teaspoons vanilla extract
1	cup (2 sticks) unsalted butter, softened		

Preheat the oven to 325°F. Grease and flour a 10-inch tube or bundt pan.
Dust the bottom of the pan with granulated sugar.

In a bowl, sift together the flour, salt, and baking soda. Set aside.

In the top of a double boiler or in a microwave, melt the chocolate.
Set aside.

In a mixing bowl, cream the butter and sugar together until light and fluffy.
Add the eggs, one at a time, beating well after each addition. Alternately, add
some of the flour mixture and some of the sour cream until incorporated. Beat
in the vanilla extract until the batter is smooth and uniformly colored.

Spoon a third of the batter evenly around the pan. Spoon or drizzle half the
chocolate as evenly as possible over the batter. Spoon another third of the batter evenly into the pan, followed by the rest of the chocolate, then the rest
of the batter.

With a table knife in one hand, cut the knife through the batter in a spiral
(like the blade of an outboard motor in water) and slowly turn the pan one rev-
olution with the other hand. (See note.)

Bake for 1 hour 20 minutes, or until a toothpick inserted in the center
comes out clean. Cool in the pan for 10 minutes, then turn out onto a rack
and cool completely.

A NOTE ABOUT SWIRLING: The idea in swirling the chocolate through the
batter is not to mix it in, but to streak the batter. Efficiency of strokes is what
you're after. Imagine how you want the swirls to look when you slice the cake,
and "draw" that pattern with your knife.

*For fancy's sake, place a small glass in the hole made by the tube and fill it with as
many flowers as guests. Accompany each slice with a flower (edibles like pansy, lilac,
honeysuckle, and borage add an exotic element).*

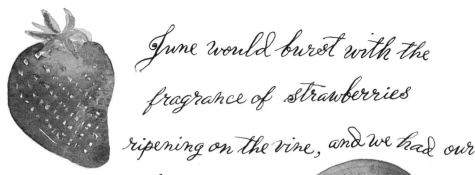

June would burst with the
fragrance of strawberries
ripening on the vine, and we had our
pick of patches.
Bett's, the closest, was
a sun-drenched paradise,
but because as many
Bett berries went
into our mouths
as our baskets,
we'd usually have to hike
down the road to
Sue's, as well.
Whatever
was left became
pick-of-the-day cake,
a splendiferous touch
to a blessed day.

Pick-of-the-Day
Fruitcake

*As sweet as summer, this dense cake holds up in any season topped
with whatever fruit is ripe—from berries to peaches to pears.*

Cake

1½ cups all-purpose flour
1 teaspoon baking powder
½ cup milk
1 teaspoon vanilla extract

½ cup (1 stick) unsalted butter, softened
1 cup granulated sugar
2 large eggs

Preheat the oven to 350°F. Grease a 9-inch springform pan.

In a bowl, sift together the flour and baking powder. Set aside.

Stir together the milk and vanilla extract. Set aside.

In a mixing bowl, cream the butter and sugar together. Add the eggs one at
a time and beat well. Alternately add the flour and the milk mixtures until
incorporated.

Pour the batter into the pan and bake for 45 to 50 minutes, or until a
toothpick inserted in the center comes out clean. Cool the cake completely in
the pan.

Topping

3 ounces cream cheese, softened
1 cup heavy cream
¼ cup confectioners' sugar
½ teaspoon grated lemon zest
1 teaspoon lemon juice
1 teaspoon vanilla extract
2 cups fresh, seasonal fruit (whole,

halved, or sliced, depending on
size; washed, well-dried; peeled,
cored, or seeded as necessary)
½ cup apricot (or other
appropriate) preserves
2 tablespoons Grand Marnier
(or other similar liqueur)

In a bowl, beat the cream cheese until fluffy. Gradually beat in the cream.
Add the sugar, lemon zest and juice, and the vanilla and beat until well combined and the mixture resembles stiff whipped cream. Spread evenly over the
cake and arrange the prepared fruit on top.

In a small saucepan, heat the preserves and liqueur, stirring until soupy.
Pass through a sieve, pressing with the back of a spoon to force as much
through as possible. Discard any solids left in the sieve.

Spoon the glaze over the fruit, coating well.

Cover and chill for at least 1 hour until set. Run a sharp knife around the
sides of the pan. Remove the sides of the pan, then the bottom.

Let the cake warm slightly before serving.

Major Henderson, the town attorney, was a frequent visitor to the farm, being Grandpa Arnet's fishing partner. The two of them would angle for a quiet eternity on the pond, and when they'd start to row in, we'd come running. The major'd jingle the change in his pocket, offering a nickel for a song — "Froggy Went A-Courtin'" every time. We'd groan, then sing, then give him a big slice of Mattie's peach coffee cake.

Peach-Almond Coffee Cake

The peach, symbol of the South, combines with the almonds for a heavenly perfumed effect.

Cake

3	medium-size ripe peaches
3	teaspoons almond extract
½	cup firmly packed light brown sugar
2	cups all-purpose flour
3	tablespoons unsalted butter, chilled
⅓	cup sliced almonds
½	cup granulated sugar
½	teaspoon baking soda
½	teaspoon baking powder
¼	teaspoon salt
½	cup (1 stick) unsalted butter, softened
½	cup sour cream or yogurt
1	large egg

Preheat the oven to 350°F. Grease an 8-inch square baking pan.

For easy skinning, drop the peaches into a pot of boiling water for 2 minutes. Remove and drop into cold water for a moment, until they are cool enough to handle. Strip off the skin, using a paring knife on any difficult spots. Slice the peaches and place in a bowl. Sprinkle them with 1 teaspoon of the almond extract and toss gently. Set aside.

In another bowl, combine the light brown sugar with ½ cup of the flour. With a pastry blender, 2 knives, or your fingers, cut in the chilled butter until the mixture resembles bread crumbs. Gently stir in the sliced almonds. Set aside.

In a medium bowl, stir together the remaining 1½ cups of flour, the granulated sugar, baking soda, baking powder, and salt. With an electric mixer on low, or by hand, blend the ingredients until thoroughly combined. Add the softened butter, sour cream or yogurt, egg, and the remaining 2 teaspoons of almond extract and mix until thoroughly moistened. The batter will be thick.

Pour the batter into the pan and spread evenly. Arrange the peach slices on top, drizzling them with any juice left in the bowl. Sprinkle the almond/crumb mixture over the top and bake for 35 to 40 minutes, or until the cake is golden brown and wiggles only slightly in the center when the pan is tapped. Serve somewhat warm or at room temperature.

☺ This cake is best made with peaches in season, but if you have a hankering for it in the winter, use the best fresh peaches you can find.

Sweatered up for a long morning under the soaring pecan trees, we'd bend to the task of gathering the fallen nuts. A bumper crop meant a hard winter ahead—at least that's what the adults would say. So we'd forage extra hard, knowing our reward would be a slice of just-baked pecan coffee cake.

Pecan Coffee Cake

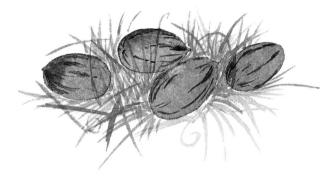

*A richer texture than most coffee cakes, the pecans in the
streusel topping become slightly toasted during baking, adding
a deliciously nutty crunch.*

Cake

1½ teaspoons ground cinnamon
½ cup firmly packed light brown
   sugar
1⅓ cups chopped pecans
1 cup all-purpose flour
1½ teaspoons baking powder
1 teaspoon baking soda

⅔ cup buttermilk
1 teaspoon vanilla extract
1 teaspoon lemon juice
10 tablespoons (1¼ sticks) unsalted
   butter, softened
⅔ cup granulated sugar
2 large eggs

Preheat the oven to 350° F. Grease an 8-inch square pan.

In a small bowl, stir together the cinnamon, light brown sugar, and nuts.
Set aside.

In another bowl, sift together the flour, baking powder, and baking soda.
Set aside.

Combine the buttermilk, vanilla extract, and lemon juice. Set aside.

In a mixing bowl, cream together the butter and granulated sugar until light
and fluffy. Add the eggs, one at a time, beating well after each addition. Add
the buttermilk mixture and combine thoroughly. Add the flour mixture and
blend until smooth.

Spread half the batter in the pan. Sprinkle half the nut mixture over it.
Spoon the rest of the batter evenly into the pan and sprinkle with the
remaining nut mixture. Bake for 40 to 45 minutes, or until a toothpick
inserted in the center comes out clean. Cool in the pan. Serve warm or at
room temperature.

*A friendly brunch offering, this one works just as well as
an afternoon tea or dessert cake.*

Grandpa Arnet died late in the fall. I remember the people coming to pay their respects. It went on all day. Mattie stayed strong throughout until my aunt Em arrived. She embraced my grandmother with one arm; the other arm bore the apple cake she had baked, probably to ease her own sorrow as much as Mattie's.

Brown Sugar-Glazed Apple Cake

Apples celebrate the fall harvest. This cake is chock-full of them and topped with a simple, old-fashioned glaze.

Cake

3   cups all-purpose flour
1   teaspoon baking soda
½   teaspoon salt
2   cups granulated sugar
1   cup vegetable oil
3   large eggs

1   teaspoon vanilla extract
1   cup chopped pecans
3   cups peeled, cored, and chopped apples (about 2 medium-to-large apples)

Preheat the oven to 350°F. Grease a 10-inch tube or bundt pan. In a bowl, sift together the flour, baking soda, and salt. Set aside.

In a mixing bowl, beat together the sugar, oil, eggs, and vanilla extract until pale and uniformly colored. Beat in the flour mixture, a third at a time. The batter will be very thick. Mix in the nuts and apples. Spoon the batter into the pan, smoothing the top. Bake for 55 minutes, or until a toothpick inserted in the center comes out clean. Cool in the pan for 10 minutes, then turn out onto a rack and cool completely before glazing.

Glaze

1   cup firmly packed light brown sugar

⅓   cup unsalted butter
⅓   cup milk

Place all the ingredients in a small saucepan. Bring to a boil and boil rapidly for 5 minutes.

Remove from the heat and stir vigorously until all the bubbles are gone. Spoon over the cake, allowing the glaze to drizzle down the sides.

NOTE: This batter can be difficult to mix because of its thickness when the last third of the flour is incorporated. The apples put a lot of moisture into the cake while it is baking and the result is pretty and flavorful—worth the extra muscle.

We always used macintosh apples for their tartness and texture, but most any apple will do. Well wrapped and refrigerated, the cake will stay fresh for up to a week.

Sunday supper under the trees — fried chicken, snap beans biscuits and gravy... This cake was another of my Dad's favorites, and if he'd had too much fried chicken to accommodate that second slice comfortably, he'd loosen his belt a notch or two.

Southern Coconut Layer Cake

A particularly Southern handcrafted beauty, ambrosial in look and taste.

Cake

- 3 large eggs, separated
- 10 tablespoons (1¼ sticks) unsalted butter, softened
- 1½ cups granulated sugar
- 1 teaspoon vanilla extract
- ⅔ cup coconut milk, canned, frozen, or fresh
- 2 cups sifted, self-rising cake flour (See note.)

Preheat the oven to 350° F. Grease and flour two 9-inch cake pans.

In a bowl, beat the egg whites until stiff, but not dry.

In another bowl, cream the butter and sugar together until light and fluffy. Add the egg yolks and beat well. Combine the coconut milk and vanilla extract and add to the yolk mixture alternately with the flour until fully combined. Fold in a third of the egg whites, then the remaining whites.

Divide the batter evenly between the pans and bake for 25 minutes, or until a toothpick inserted in the center of each layer comes out clean. Cool in the pans for 10 minutes, then turn out onto racks and cool completely.

Glaze

½ cup coconut milk, canned, frozen, or fresh

¼ cup granulated sugar
½ teaspoon vanilla extract

In a small saucepan combine the coconut milk and sugar. Stir constantly over medium-high heat until the sugar is melted. Add the vanilla extract.

Starting with the layers top-side-down on the racks, pierce the layers all over with a toothpick. Brush the bottoms and sides with the glaze. After a few minutes, repeat.

Turn one layer over onto the serving plate. Invert the second layer onto the first one's rack. Pierce the tops with a toothpick. Brush the glaze over the tops and sides. Repeat after a few minutes until all the glaze has been used. Let sit for 30 minutes before frosting.

Frosting

¾ cup granulated sugar
¼ cup water
1 tablespoon light corn syrup
1 teaspoon vanilla extract
Pinch of salt

2 large egg whites
Pinch of cream of tartar
2 cups grated fresh or frozen unsweetened coconut

Combine all the ingredients except the coconut in the top of a double boiler. With an electric mixer or by hand beat to combine. Place the frosting over rapidly boiling water and beat on high speed until soft peaks form, 3 to 5 minutes.

Pour the frosting into a large bowl and beat until stiff enough to spread on the cake. Generously frost the bottom layer and sprinkle with ½ cup of the coconut. Place the top layer on the bottom layer and frost the top and sides. Sprinkle the remaining 1½ cups of coconut all over the frosting.

NOTE: You can substitute 2 cups sifted cake flour (non-self-rising) sifted 3 times with 2 teaspoons of baking powder and ¼ teaspoon of salt.

Dip your cake knife in water between slices for neat wedges.

When Mom needed to divert Dad's attention, she'd rely on this cake. I've seen it minimize the impact of an extravagant purchase or a bent fender. Once or twice I even managed to parley its harmonious effects into a bigger allowance. After all, the hummingbird is the harbinger of good fortune and well~being.

Hummingbird Cake

A long-standing favorite in the South, this cake is as delicate as the bird for which it was named.

Cake

3 cups all-purpose flour	1 cup vegetable oil
2 cups granulated sugar	1½ teaspoons vanilla extract
1 teaspoon baking soda	One 8-ounce can crushed pineapple
1 teaspoon salt	with juice
1 teaspoon ground cinnamon	1 cup chopped pecans
3 large eggs	2 cups chopped bananas

Preheat the oven to 350°F. Grease and flour three 9-inch cake pans.

In a large mixing bowl, combine the flour, sugar, baking soda, salt, and cinnamon. Add the eggs and oil and stir until all the dry ingredients are moistened. Do not beat! Stir in the vanilla extract, pineapple with juice, pecans, and bananas.

Spoon the batter into the pans and spread evenly. Bake for 25 to 30 minutes, or until a toothpick inserted in the center of each layer comes out clean. (See note.)

Cool in the pans for 10 minutes, then remove the layers and cool completely on racks.

Frosting

One 8-ounce package cream cheese, softened	One 16-ounce package confectioners' sugar, sifted
½ cup (1 stick) unsalted butter, softened	1 teaspoon vanilla extract
	½ cup chopped pecans

In a small mixing bowl, combine the cream cheese and butter, beating until smooth. Add the confectioners' sugar and vanilla extract, and beat until light and fluffy.

Spread the frosting between the layers and on the top and sides of the cake. Sprinkle the pecans over the top.

NOTE: When baking 3 layers at one time, one layer may be done as much as 2 to 5 minutes before another. Therefore, test all for doneness, removing each at the appropriate time.

⑨For an impressive and touching gift, buy a fancy doily and a cake box (available at cooking supply stores), to cage the hummingbird, and tie it all up with ribbon.

H.L. Perry lived across the road. He drove big bright Cadillacs (traded in yearly), and was known for his girth, his abundant good humor, and his extensive liquor cabinet—especially the unlabeled bottles he got from less than conventional sources. This was his favorite cake. It's dedicated to H.L. and all who've made an art of living large.

Lane Cake

Six layers of Southern comfort, this cake is often served at Christmas.

Cake

3½ cups cake flour
2 teaspoons baking powder
¼ teaspoon salt
1 cup milk
1 teaspoon vanilla extract

8 large egg whites (reserve yolks for filling)
1 cup (2 sticks) unsalted butter, softened
1½ cups granulated sugar

Preheat the oven to 350°F. Grease three 8-inch cake pans, line the bottoms with baking parchment or wax paper, grease the paper, and dust with flour.

In a bowl, sift together the flour, baking powder, and salt. Set aside.

Combine the milk and vanilla extract. Set aside.

In another bowl, beat the egg whites until stiff, but not dry. Set aside.

In a mixing bowl, cream the butter and sugar together until light and fluffy. Starting and ending with the flour mixture, add some of the flour mixture to the batter alternately with some of the milk mixture until completely incorporated. Fold in a third of the egg whites until well combined. Fold in the remaining whites. Divide the batter evenly among the pans.

Bake for 30 to 35 minutes, or until a toothpick inserted in the center of each layer comes out clean. Cool in the pans for 10 minutes, then turn out onto racks. Remove the paper and cool completely.

With a sharp knife, slice each layer in half horizontally, making 6 layers.

Filling

½	cup (1 stick) unsalted butter, softened	1	cup raisins
		1	cup chopped pecans
1	cup granulated sugar	¾	cup dry white wine
8	large egg yolks	1	teaspoon vanilla extract

In a bowl, cream the butter and sugar together. Add the egg yolks and beat until light and fluffy. Mix in the remaining ingredients and transfer the mixture to the top of a double boiler set over simmering water. Cook, stirring often, until thick. Cool before spreading between the 6 cake layers.

Frosting

2	tablespoons all-purpose flour		unsalted butter, softened
⅔	cup milk	⅔	cup granulated sugar
10	tablespoons (1¼ sticks)	1	teaspoon vanilla extract

Place the flour in a small saucepan over medium-high heat. Gradually whisk in the milk. Continue to whisk constantly until the mixture thickens and all the small bubbles on top disappear. Remove from the heat and cool to room temperature.

In a bowl, cream the butter and sugar together until fluffy. Add the vanilla extract, then the cooled milk/flour mixture. Beat on high until the frosting is the consistency of whipped cream and all the sugar is dissolved. DO NOT OVERBEAT. Spread on the top and sides of the cake.

⊚ At specialty food stores, one can purchase wonderful and simple cake decorations such as crystalized flowers (violets, rosebuds, and mint), colored sparkling sugars, colored sanding sugars, rock crystals, silver and gold dragees, and chocolate curls.

Remedy for a Lonely Heart

one cherished teapot
two place settings - preferably heirloom
china and silver
a spray of favorite flowers
one antique tablecloth, ironed
one whole Bête Noire

Bête Noire

Not an ounce of flour in this one, and it's wantonly rich.

Cake

12 ounces good-quality bittersweet
or semisweet chocolate
¾ cup (1½ sticks) unsalted butter
6 large eggs, separated

Pinch of cream of tartar
½ cup confectioners' sugar
Whipped cream (optional)

Preheat the oven to 300°F. Grease a 9-inch cake pan and cover the bottom with a round of baking parchment or wax paper. Grease the paper.

Boil a kettle of water.

In the top of a double boiler set over simmering water, melt the chocolate and butter. When smooth, remove from the heat and whisk in the egg yolks until thoroughly combined. Pour the mixture into a large bowl.

In a separate bowl, beat the egg whites with the cream of tartar until stiff. Add the sugar and continue beating until stiff and well combined. Gently fold a third of the egg whites into the chocolate mixture. Then fold in the rest.

Scrape the batter into the pan, smoothing the top. Place the pan in a larger pan and pour in the boiling water to come halfway up the sides of the cake pan. Carefully place in the preheated oven and bake for 35 to 40 minutes, or until a knife inserted in the center of the cake comes out clean.

Remove the cake pan from the pan of water and cool in its pan for 10 minutes on a rack. Run a knife around the sides and turn the cake out onto a wax-paper-covered plate or a baking sheet. Remove the wax paper from the bottom of the cake, cover with a serving plate, and flip over again.

Cool to room temperature. Serve with whipped cream, if desired. Store, covered, at room temperature.

☞ *Always use the finest dark chocolate available such as Ghirardelli or Lindt.*

The cake pedestal, shrine of the batter arts, can raise the humblest attempt to glorious heights. Ours often held this classic chocolate cake... but not for long. By day 3 there'd be nothing left but a few crumbs under a dome of glass.

Very Moist Chocolate Layer Cake

This is cake for those who can never get enough chocolate. And with it come memories of birthdays gone by.

Cake

1 cup milk

4 ounces unsweetened chocolate

2 cups all-purpose flour

½ teaspoon salt

⅓ cup hot water

1 teaspoon baking soda

2 teaspoons vanilla extract

1 cup firmly packed dark brown sugar

1 cup granulated sugar

1 cup vegetable shortening (Crisco)

3 large eggs

In a small saucepan, heat the milk until bubbles begin to form around the edges. Remove from the heat, add the chocolate, cover, and set aside for 5 minutes. Stir until there are no large lumps. (Don't worry if the chocolate remains suspended as small particles in the milk.) Set aside to cool to luke-warm.

Preheat the oven to 350°F. Grease three 9-inch cake pans. Line the bottoms with rounds of baking parchment or wax paper. Grease the paper.

In a bowl, sift together the flour and salt. Set aside.

Combine the hot water and the baking soda. Stir to dissolve, then set aside.

In a bowl, cream together the brown and white sugars with the shortening until well combined. Add the eggs, one at a time, beating well after each addition. Starting and ending with the flour mixture, add some of the flour, then some of the milk/chocolate mixture alternately to the batter until completely incorporated. Add the soda water and vanilla extract. Beat until well combined.

Divide the batter equally among the pans and spread it evenly. Bake for 30 minutes, or until a toothpick inserted in the center of each layer comes out clean. Cool in the pans on racks for 10 minutes, then turn out onto the racks. Remove the paper and cool completely.

Icing

2 cups granulated sugar	2 ounces unsweetened chocolate
¼ cup light corn syrup	¼ teaspoon salt
½ cup milk	1 teaspoon vanilla extract
½ cup (1 stick) unsalted butter	

Place all the ingredients except the vanilla extract in a saucepan. Cook over low heat until everything is melted. Bring rapidly to a boil and boil for a minute or so, or until the mixture reaches 220°F. on a candy thermometer, or reaches the soft-ball stage. (See note.)

Remove from the heat. Place in a small mixing bowl and beat on medium speed until cooled slightly. Add the vanilla extract. Increase the speed and beat just until the icing is of spreading consistency. Spread icing between cooled layers and on the sides and the top of the cake, working fast before the icing sets. (It will thicken more as you spread it on the cake.)

NOTE: The soft-ball stage is reached when a bit of the mixture dropped into cold water forms a ball, which when pinched is soft, but holds together.

*۞ This miraculous icing sets up smoothly and encases the cake
in a perfect chocolate coating.*

Thanksgiving should be a feast of
blessings. Ours was, though celebrated with
conspicuous razzle-dazzle. Against the hushed
colors of winter, the good silver and company
dishes sparkled. The roast bird steaming on
his oversize platter appropriated first
honors—which the Cranberry Pecan Cake always
captured at the end of the meal.

Cranberry-Pecan Cake

*Yankee Cranberries add a rosy punch to this rare eggless cake.
Served with warm hard sauce it is especially suitable for
holiday entertaining.*

Cake

1 cup all-purpose flour	¼ cup evaporated milk
1½ teaspoons baking powder	¼ cup water
½ teaspoon salt	1 cup fresh or frozen raw
½ cup granulated sugar	cranberries (See note.)
1½ tablespoons unsalted butter, melted	½ cup chopped pecans

Preheat the oven to 350°F. Grease an 8-inch square pan.

In a bowl, sift together the flour, baking powder, and salt. Set aside.

Place the sugar in a bowl. Stir in the melted butter, moistening all the sugar. Stir in the milk and water, then the flour mixture, until incorporated. Fold in the cranberries and pecans and spread into the pan. Smooth out the batter.

Bake for 35 to 40 minutes, or until the top is lightly browned and a toothpick inserted in the center comes out clean.

Serve warm from the pan.

Hard Sauce

¼ cup (½ stick) unsalted butter	1 teaspoon vanilla extract
1 cup granulated sugar	2 tablespoons Cognac or brandy
½ cup evaporated milk	(optional)

In a small saucepan over low heat, melt the butter and add the sugar. Add the milk and bring to a boil, beating all the while. Add the vanilla and stir in the Cognac or brandy, if desired, and drizzle over the warm cake.

NOTE: If using frozen cranberries, do not defrost.

☙ *Put this cake in the oven just before you sit down to dinner and it will be ready to serve warm when it is time for dessert.*

When company came, Mom baked company cake, a particular favorite of the un-invited—my sister and me. Sneaking down after bedtime, making sure the coast was clear, we'd grab our share and, safely back, fight over whether to alternate nibbles of cake with icing or finish the icing first and leave the delicate heart of the cake for last. Truly, either method was sublime sitting on the dark staircase listening to the upwellings of tinkling glasses and ripples of adult laughter.

Brownstone Front Cake

[Company Cake]

This charmingly Victorian construction of light chocolate layers is covered in a rich caramel icing.

Cake

½ cup water
2 ounces unsweetened chocolate
1 teaspoon baking soda
1 cup (2 sticks) unsalted butter, softened

2 cups granulated sugar
3 large eggs
3 cups sifted all-purpose flour
1 cup buttermilk
1 teaspoon vanilla extract

In a small saucepan, heat the water until it begins to steam. Remove from the heat and add the chocolate and baking soda. Cover and let stand for 5 minutes. Stir until smooth. Cool to room temperature.

Preheat the oven to 350°F. Grease and flour three 9-inch cake pans.

In a bowl, cream the butter and sugar together until fluffy. Add the eggs, one at a time, beating well after each addition. Beat in the cooled chocolate mixture. Starting and ending with the flour mixture, add some of the flour alternately with some of the buttermilk to the batter until completely incorporated. Mix well. Beat in the vanilla extract and continue to beat, scraping the sides, until the batter is a uniform color.

Divide the batter equally among the pans and bake for 25 to 30 minutes, or until a toothpick inserted in the center of each layer comes out clean. Start the frosting while the cake is baking.

Icing

1 cup (2 sticks) unsalted butter
2 cups granulated sugar

1 cup evaporated milk
1 teaspoon vanilla extract

In a 10-inch cast-iron or other heavy skillet, melt the butter over medium-low heat. Add the sugar and evaporated milk. Raise the heat to medium-high and bring to a boil, stirring constantly.

When the icing is boiling, lower the heat and simmer for about 45 minutes or longer, or until it registers 220°F. on a candy thermometer (soft-ball stage). Remove from the heat and cool until you can put your hand on the bottom of the pan. Pour into a small mixing bowl and beat until thick enough to spread comfortably. Spread the icing between the layers and on the top and sides of the cake. The icing will thicken further as it is being spread—if some runs down, spread it back on the sides until it stays.

⊚ *This icing will not set in damp weather, so bake the cake on a clear day!*

Tiered, iced, and decorated
with sprigs of holly, this cake served
the guest lists of two December Gourley
weddings—my sister's and mine. Mom
admits that our family stole the cake for
our weddings from its traditional Christmas
presentation. Reinvented it, I'd say.

CAKEWALK

Christmas Fruitcake
[Wedding Cake]

*Not the kind of fruitcake you're likely to receive
in the mail. This one's dense but cakier, and the black walnuts
add an unexpected taste!*

Cake

2 cups (about 8 ounces) pecan halves	2 cups sifted all-purpose flour
2 cups (about 8 ounces) black walnut pieces (See note.)	1 cup (2 sticks) unsalted butter, softened
2 cups (about 1 pound) candied cherries	1⅔ cups granulated sugar
	5 large eggs
	1 cup shredded moist coconut

Place the oven rack at the lowest level and preheat the oven to 275°F. Grease a 10-inch tube pan, line it with baking parchment or wax paper. Grease the paper. Have a second, larger and shallower pan ready for the tube pan to sit in. Put a kettle of water on to heat.

Place the nuts and cherries in a large bowl. Sprinkle them with ⅔ cup of the flour and stir to coat them thoroughly. Set aside.

In a mixing bowl, cream the butter until light and fluffy. Add the sugar gradually, creaming together well. Add the eggs, one at a time, beating well after each addition. Add the remaining 1⅓ cups of flour and beat it in thoroughly. By hand, fold in the nuts and cherries and the coconut until well mixed.

Spread the batter in the tube pan. Cover it with foil and crimp around the edges to seal. Place the tube pan in the larger pan and pour 1 to 1½ inches of hot water into the outer pan. Bake for 3 hours. Remove the foil and bake for an additional 15 minutes. The cake is done when a wire tester or toothpick inserted near the center comes out with no crumbs clinging to it. Cool in the pan for 15 minutes, then turn out onto a rack. Remove the wax paper and cool the cake completely.

⊚Adding more spirit to the holidays means planning ahead. Wrap the cake tightly in several layers of cheesecloth. Soak the cloth with bourbon, rum, or Cognac. Place the cake in an airtight container. "Ripen" it for one month in a cool place, drizzling it with additional liquor as the cloth dries out.

If ever there was a cake that separated the serious contenders from the also-rans, it was this one. My Aunt Wadie tried and tried, and each attempt was tasty enough, but only indomitable Willa Mae succeeded in creating the vision a Rocky Mountain fruit cake should be.

Rocky Mountain Fruitcake

Named for the rugged Rockies, this cake should resemble a mountain of fruit under a blanket of snow. The challenge is well worth the effort, but if serving to impress, practice first!

Cake

3 cups all-purpose flour
2 teaspoons baking powder
1 cup milk
1 teaspoon vanilla extract

1 cup (2 sticks) unsalted butter, softened
2 cups granulated sugar
4 large eggs

Preheat the oven to 350°F. Grease and flour three 9-inch cake pans.

In a bowl, sift together the flour and baking powder. Set aside.

Combine the milk and vanilla extract. Set aside.

In a mixing bowl, cream together the butter and sugar. Add the eggs, one at a time, beating well after each addition. Add some of the flour mixture and some of the milk mixture alternately, mixing well after each, until all is incorporated.

Pour the batter evenly into the pans. Bake for 25 to 30 minutes, or until a toothpick inserted in the center of each layer comes out clean. Cool in the pans on racks for 10 minutes, then turn out onto the racks and cool completely.

Frosting

1 cup (2 sticks) unsalted butter
1½ cups firmly packed dark brown sugar
⅓ cup milk
1 cup chopped moist dates
1 cup chopped moist dried figs

1 cup chopped moist raisins
1 cup shredded moist coconut
2 oranges, peeled, seeded, membranes removed, flesh chopped
1 cup chopped pecans

In a heavy 2½- or 3-quart saucepan, combine the butter, sugar, and milk. Melt the butter over low heat, stirring to dissolve the sugar.

When the butter has melted, add the remaining ingredients, stir to blend, raise the heat to medium-high, and boil, scraping the bottom frequently to prevent scorching, until the mixture registers 220°F. on a candy thermometer or reaches the soft-ball stage (5 to 10 minutes). Remove from the heat.

Pour the frosting into a large mixing bowl and beat on high speed for 2 minutes to cool slightly. Spread the frosting between the layers and on the top and sides of the cake. The frosting will continue to thicken after it is spread.

☺A winter's cake and very sweet, best pair it with a proper cup of tea.

Who was Lady Baltimore?

Elegant, rich and complex

Forever patient and kind

Her great skirts whooshed as she walked Her hair ~ tall and sculpted ~ was unmovable even in the wind.

Adored by children (to whom she dedicated this cake)

Lord Baltimore's wife

Lady Baltimore

Rum gives a kick to this version of the classic. With its pure white icing, it's purely delicious.

Cake

3	cups sifted cake flour
2	teaspoons baking powder
¼	teaspoon salt
1	cup milk
½	cup (1 stick) unsalted butter, softened

1½	teaspoons vanilla extract
1½	cups granulated sugar
5	large egg whites, at room temperature (reserve yolks for filling)

Preheat the oven to 350°F. Grease three 8-inch cake pans, line the bottoms with rounds of baking parchment or wax paper. Grease the paper.

In a bowl, sift together the sifted cake flour, baking powder, and salt. Set aside.

Combine the milk and vanilla extract.

In a mixing bowl, cream together the butter and sugar until light and fluffy. Alternately add some of the milk, then some of the flour mixture to the butter and sugar, beating well after each addition, until completely combined.

If using a mixer, change or clean and dry the mixer blades and beat the egg whites until they hold stiff peaks. Fold a third of the egg whites into the batter. When incorporated, gently fold in the remaining whites until thoroughly combined. Scrape the batter into the pans and spread out evenly.

Bake for 25 to 30 minutes, or until a toothpick inserted in the center of each layer comes out clean. Cool in the pans on racks for 10 minutes, then run a sharp knife around the sides of the pans and turn out onto the racks. Remove the paper and cool completely. Roast the almonds for the filling before turning the oven off.

Filling

1	cup currants	1	tablespoon grated orange zest
⅔	cup white rum	5	egg yolks
1	cup granulated sugar	¾	cup roasted sliced almonds

Place the currants in a small bowl and cover with the rum. Soak for at least 30 minutes. Reserving the currants, drain off the rum and place it in the top of a double boiler set over simmering water, along with the sugar, orange zest, and egg yolks. Whisk until smooth, then continue to stir constantly until thickened. Add the reserved currants and the almonds. Mix thoroughly and spread between the cake layers.

Frosting

¾	cup granulated sugar	1	egg white, at room temperature
¼	cup water		Pinch of cream of tartar
2	teaspoons light corn syrup	12	candied cherries, for garnish
½	teaspoon vanilla extract		(optional)

Combine all the ingredients except the cherries in the top of a double boiler. With an electric mixer, beat at high speed for 1 minute. Place over rapidly boiling water and beat at high speed continuously until soft peaks form (2 or 3 minutes). Pour the frosting into a bowl and continue to beat on high until stiff enough to spread.

Frost the sides and the top of the cake. Garnish with candied cherries, if desired.

To roast sliced almonds, spread them out in a single layer on a shallow pan and cook in a preheated 350°F. oven for 8 to 10 minutes, tossing twice, until browned. They will continue to darken after they're removed from the oven. Cool on a plate or paper towels.

A great spirit
resides on the farm.
I can hear it: high,
choral, in bird song.
I can smell it in the
grass, in the woods,
by the river, in the garden. I can taste it
in this sweet and rich nut cake.

Walnut Cake with Chocolate Whipped Cream Topping

Replacing flour with ground walnuts keeps this cake dense and moist. The chocolate topping is as smooth as silk.

Cake

2	cups walnut pieces	¼	teaspoon salt
2	tablespoons all-purpose flour	1	cup granulated sugar
6	large eggs, separated, at room temperature	1	teaspoon vanilla extract
		¼	teaspoon cream of tartar

Preheat the oven to 350°F. Grease three 8-inch cake pans, line the bottoms with rounds of parchment or wax paper. Grease the paper.

Place the nuts, flour, and salt in the bowl of a food processor fitted with a steel blade and process until finely ground. The mixture should look like bread crumbs. Set aside.

In a bowl, beat the egg yolks with the sugar until the mixture lightens slightly in color and thickens. Add the vanilla extract and beat until well combined. Mix in the nut mixture by hand until well combined. (The batter will be very thick.) Set aside.

In another bowl, beat the egg whites with the cream of tartar until they hold stiff peaks.

With a large balloon whisk or a rubber spatula, fold a third of the whites into the egg/nut mixture, incorporating thoroughly. Fold in the remaining whites gently, until thoroughly combined.

Divide the batter equally among the pans. Bake for 30 to 35 minutes, or until each layer springs back when touched lightly in the center. Remove from the oven and set the pans on racks. With a sharp knife, cut around the outside edge. Cool for 10 minutes, then turn out onto racks, remove the paper, and cool completely. Meanwhile, begin the frosting.

Chocolate Whipped Cream Topping

¼ pound good-quality semisweet chocolate, in pieces

2 cups heavy cream

1 teaspoon vanilla extract

½ cup chopped walnuts

In the top of a double boiler set over simmering water or in the microwave, melt the chocolate with ½ cup of the cream. Stir until the chocolate is completely melted and the mixture is smooth. Cool to room temperature.

While the chocolate cools, chill a mixing bowl, beaters, and the remaining 1½ cups of the cream.

When ready to frost, beat the cream until beater marks begin to show. Add the chocolate mixture and vanilla extract and continue to beat until the mixture forms soft peaks when the beaters are raised.

Spread the topping between the layers and on the top and sides of the cake. Sprinkle the nuts over the top, pressing them in slightly, just enough that they stick. Refrigerate. Remove 1 hour before serving and serve at room temperature.

My third-grade class hosted our school's cake-walk. A game board of squares was drawn around the room. All our moms donated cakes, which were displayed on cloth-covered desktops as the leader started up the record player (also donated). When the music stopped, and if I was lucky enough to land on a prize square, I always chose the Krazy Kake my mom had made.

Krazy Kake

A great choice when facing a crowd. This chocolate sheet cake gets 2 layers of icing that mix and bubble into some pretty "krazy" designs.

Cake

3	cups all-purpose flour		2	cups water, at room temperature
2	cups granulated sugar		2	tablespoons white vinegar
⅓	cup unsweetened cocoa powder		1	teaspoon vanilla extract
2	teaspoons baking soda		¾	cup vegetable oil
1	teaspoon salt			

Preheat the oven to 350°F.

In a mixing bowl, sift together the flour, sugar, cocoa, baking soda, and salt three times. Spread the mixture in an ungreased 13 by 9 by 2-inch baking pan.

In another bowl, combine the water, vinegar, and vanilla extract. Pour over the dry ingredients in the pan. Then pour the oil over all.

Using a fork carefully, making sure to keep the ingredients in the pan, stir everything together until the mixture is a uniform color and has no obvious lumps.

Bake for 30 to 35 minutes, or until a toothpick inserted in the center comes out clean. Cool completely in the pan before icing.

First Icing

2½ tablespoons all-purpose flour
½ cup milk
½ cup granulated sugar
½ cup (1 stick) unsalted butter, softened

Place the flour in a small saucepan over medium-high heat. Slowly whisk in the milk and continue whisking until the mixture has thickened enough to see whisk marks. Remove from the heat and cool to room temperature.

In a mixing bowl, cream the butter and sugar together until light and fluffy. Add the cooled milk/flour mixture and beat until the icing has the consistency of whipped cream and all the sugar is dissolved.

Spread over the cooled cake in the pan.

Second Icing

½ cup (1 stick) unsalted butter
1 cup granulated sugar
2 tablespoons unsweetened cocoa powder
¼ cup milk
2 tablespoons corn syrup
1 teaspoon vanilla extract

Place all the ingredients except the vanilla extract in a saucepan. Set over medium heat until the butter is melted, stirring well to combine. Raise the heat and bring to a boil. When at full boil (boiling all over, not just around the edges), let boil for one minute undisturbed. Remove from the heat, add the vanilla extract, and beat until thick. Pour immediately over the first icing.

Try this icing on any basic cake when you want to give a new look to an old staple.

There never was a cake like this...
handed down and down... touched by
each spirit along the way... from
Mattie to Bett, from Willa Mae
to Dorothy, from Wadie to Sue,
from Elouise to Pam to Robbin, and
awaiting Hannah and Luke, to see
what they will make of it.

Red Velvet Cake

[Hand-Me-Down Cake]

The magic of food coloring turns this cake a vivid red. Some other magic gives it its sumptuous, velvety texture. The combination is a knockout.

Cake

2½ cups all-purpose flour
2 tablespoons unsweetened cocoa powder
1 teaspoon baking soda
½ teaspoon salt
1 tablespoon red food coloring (yes, 1 tablespoon)

1 cup buttermilk
1 cup (2 sticks) unsalted butter, softened
1½ cups granulated sugar
3 large eggs
1 teaspoon vanilla extract
1 tablespoon white vinegar

Preheat the oven to 350°F. Grease and flour two 9-inch cake pans.

In a bowl, sift together the flour, cocoa, baking soda, and salt. Set aside. Combine the buttermilk and the food coloring. Set aside.

In a mixing bowl, cream together the butter and sugar. Add the eggs, one at a time, and beat until thoroughly combined. Alternately, add some of the flour mixture, then some of the buttermilk mixture, until all is incorporated. Add the vanilla extract and vinegar, and beat until a uniform color is achieved.

Spread the batter evenly in the pans and bake for 30 minutes, or until a toothpick inserted into the center of each layer comes out clean. Cool in the pans for 10 minutes, then turn out onto racks and cool completely.

Frosting

3 tablespoons all-purpose flour
1 cup (2 sticks) unsalted butter, softened

1 cup milk
1 cup granulated sugar
1 teaspoon vanilla extract

Place the flour in a small saucepan over medium-high heat and gradually whisk in the milk. Continue to whisk constantly until the mixture becomes thick and all the small bubbles on top disappear. Remove from the heat and cool to room temperature. (If you are in a hurry, you can place the pan in the